an easy-read ACTIVITY book

MAKING SPACE PUPPETS

written and illustrated by
Dave Ross

Franklin Watts
New York/London/Toronto/Sydney
1980

**To Frank,
for continuing guidance
and support**

R.L. 2.9 Spache Revised Formula

Library of Congress Cataloging in Publication Data

Ross, Dave
  Making space puppets.

  (An Easy-read activity book)
  SUMMARY: Directions for using material found
around the house to create a variety of puppets with
space themes.
  1. Puppet making—Juvenile literature. [1. Puppet
making] I. Title. II. Title: Space puppets.
TT174.7.R658   745.592'24   80-11846
ISBN 0-531-04143-3

CONTENTS

4

For hundreds of years people all over the world have made and used puppets.

This book shows you how to make all kinds of space puppets from things you can find around the house.

Space puppets are fun to make and fun to use. Making them is something you can do by yourself or with a friend. Then you can put on space puppet shows.

MAKE SPACE PUPPETS OUT OF YOUR HAND

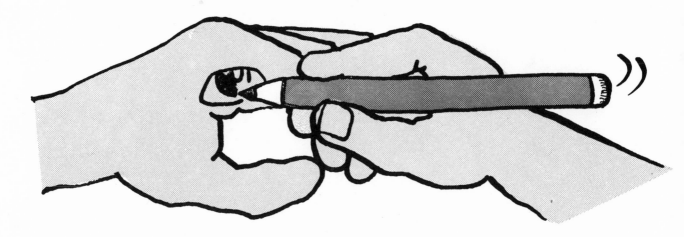

With a water-based magic marker, draw a scary eye on the knuckle of your first finger. Then make a fist. When you move your thumb, the space creature will open and close its mouth.

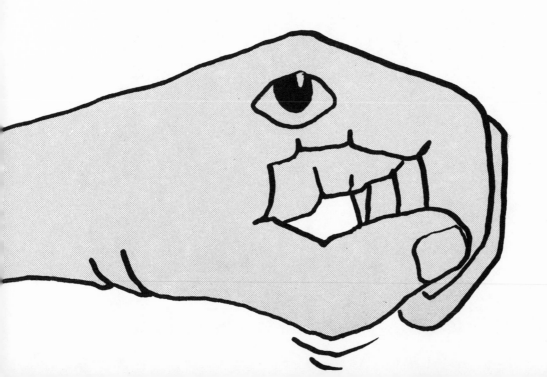

Decorate your space creature! Wrap string or woolen yarn around your first finger and thumb. Make fangs out of white tape.

You can also use pieces of cloth, pipe cleaners, and ribbons to dress up your space creature.

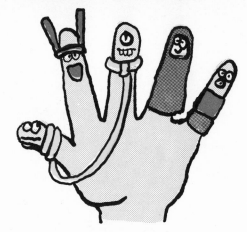

FINGER PUPPETS

Your hand can be a home for a whole family of space puppets!

Use a water-based magic marker or bits of tape to make different faces.

Tie a piece of string from your middle finger to your thumb. Your thumb becomes a space pet!

Use pipe cleaners to make horns or wings. Tape them on.

You can use one finger from an old rubber glove to make a space suit.

If you wear a ring, make it into something special, like a collar!

LET YOUR FINGERS DO THE WALKING!

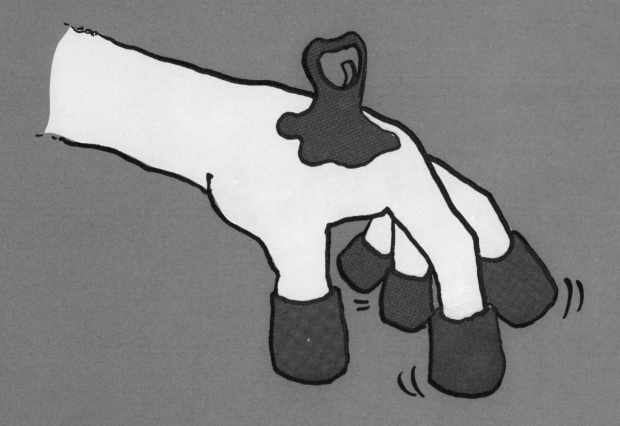

Make an eye and four feet from pieces of clay. Attach them to your hand.

If you use both hands, you can have a hand puppet monster war!

9

A WALKING HAND ROBOT

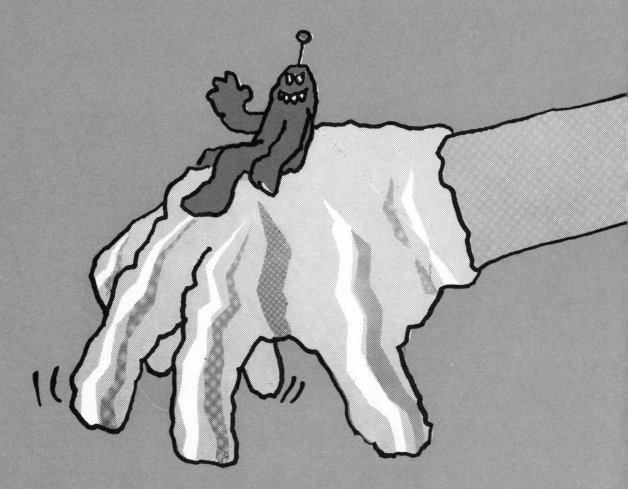

Shape tin foil around your hand to make a walking hand robot. Then make an alien from clay and attach it to the foil on top of your hand. Your fingers become a robot that will take the alien on a fantastic journey!

10

A PAPER PLATE CHOMPER

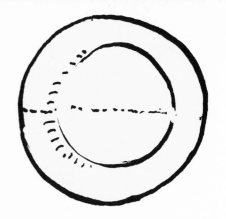

Fold the paper plate in half.

Use some scrap paper to make eyes and a nose. Cut them out and fold a small tab on each piece.

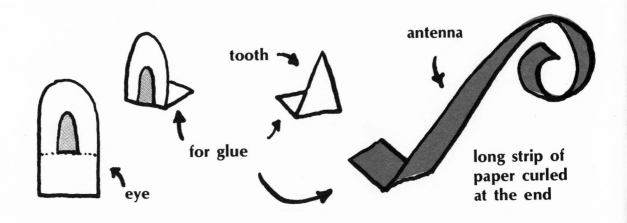

tooth

antenna

for glue

eye

long strip of
paper curled
at the end

Squeeze the fold with your hand. The puppet will open and close its mouth!

CRAZY PLANET STICK PUPPET

Cut a bunch of shapes from pieces of foil or paper. Choose one of the shapes and attach it to a strip of cardboard or a flat stick. Paste on eyes, some noses, or a mouth made from small pieces of paper.

Take a large piece of paper. Cut it into a crazy planet shape. Make a wavy slit through it. Don't cut the slit too close to the edge.

Paste the small shapes on the planet. These can be plants, animals, or houses.

Slide the stick end of your puppet through the slit. You can take your stick puppet for a walk around a crazy planet!

HUNGRY CREATURE

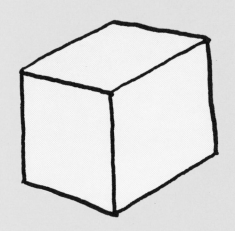

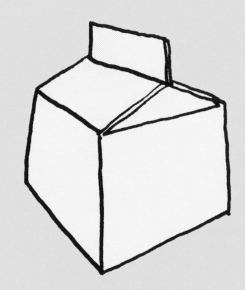

Take a small box or milk carton. Cut around three sides of the box. Bend the two halves of the box back so that the side you didn't cut becomes a hinge.

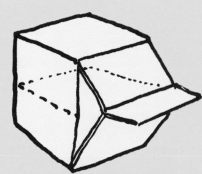

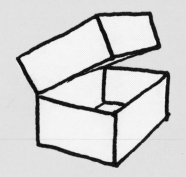

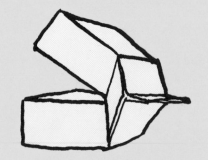

Add new shapes to your hungry creature!
Cut out details from scrap paper and paste
them on the sides of the box.

Use the hinge to open and close the
creature's mouth. Cut pictures of creature food
from old magazines. That's the only kind of
food it will eat!

PAPER BAG SPACE CADET

Slide your hand inside a folded lunch bag or small paper bag. By opening and closing your hand you can make a mouth that moves.

Paste on eyes, eyelashes, and teeth cut out
from bits of paper. Use a magic marker to add
details.

Make springy arms and legs by folding a
strip of paper back and forth like an accordian.

A MITTEN COSMIC MONSTER

Make a quick and easy cosmic monster from an old mitten. Find some scraps of old cloth or paper, and make a mouth, eyes, and a nose. Glue the scraps onto the mitten.

18

FIVE-LEGGED MOON CRAWLER

Make a cloth ball by stuffing a big piece of cloth with smaller pieces. Sew the stuffed ball onto an old glove. Sew on buttons for eyes. Or cut the eyes out of paper and glue them on. Make tufts of yarn from wool. Push a pipe cleaner through the crawler's head.

PAPIER-MÂCHÉ PUPPET HEADS

To make papier-mâché mix:
Use either one cup of wallpaper paste with two cups of water. Or boil one cup of white flour with two cups of water until it makes a paste.

Next, you will need a form to build the head over. A small blown-up balloon or some crumpled-up newspaper will do. The form should be about the size of a grapefruit.

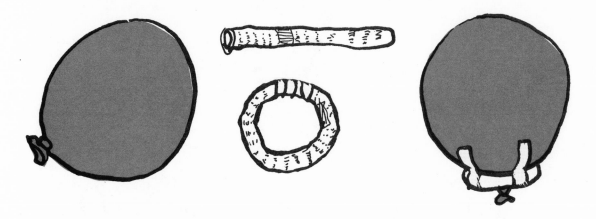

Tape a collar made of rolled-up paper onto the bottom of the form. Make sure the collar is just big enough to slide three fingers through.

Tear some newspaper into long, narrow strips. Dip the strips into the papier-mâché mix. Cover the form with several layers that cross each other. Let this dry overnight.

Use small wads of paper to make eyes, horns, ears and a mouth. Tape these onto the head. Add two more layers of paper strips dipped in the paste. Let the whole thing dry overnight.

Push your fingers through the collar and into the head. If you used a balloon, it is all right to pop it and take it out. Paint the head with tempera or other water-based paints. Use lots of different paints.

CLOTH BODY SPACE PUPPETS

Now you can make a body for your papier-mâché head or you can make a whole hand puppet out of cloth.

First make a pattern. On a piece of paper, trace an outline of your hand. Then draw another outline that is 2 inches (5 cm) bigger than the one you first drew.

Cut out along the outer line. This is your pattern. Trace the pattern on two pieces of cloth. Cut out the two pieces. Then glue or sew the two pieces together.

Cut details out of other pieces of cloth. Glue or sew them on to the body.

If the cloth body is for a papier-mâché head, cut the top off just above the arms. Glue the opening around the neck of the papier-mâché head. Attach it to the body.

Put your thumb in one arm of the puppet, and your smallest finger in the other arm. Your middle three fingers should fit inside the head. Now you can begin your puppet show!

SOCKO THE SPACE SNAKE

Find an old sock that has no mate. With some cardboard and a couple of buttons, you can turn the sock into Socko the Space Snake.

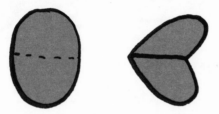

Cut an egg shape about the size of your hand out of stiff paper or cardboard.

Fold the piece of cardboard in half.

Glue this onto the toe end of the sock. Let it dry overnight.

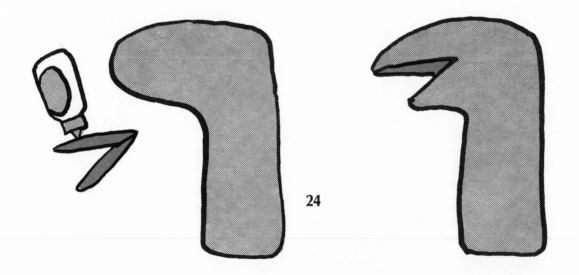

Sew on buttons for eyes, or glue on scraps of cloth.

You can make teeth from small pieces of cloth or paper. Put a drop of glue on the teeth and attach them.

Add short pieces of woolen yarn or scraps of cloth cut in strips. These can be whiskers or antennae. Or they can be anything you want them to be.

A PUPPET THAT MOVES

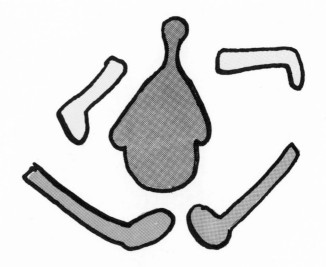

You will need
cardboard
paper fasteners
string
two short sticks

Cut the cardboard into five pieces: two arms, two legs, and a body.

If you want the arms or the legs to be springy, use a zigzag fold.

Use the paper fasteners to attach the arms and legs. Wiggle the arms and legs until they are loose enough to move.

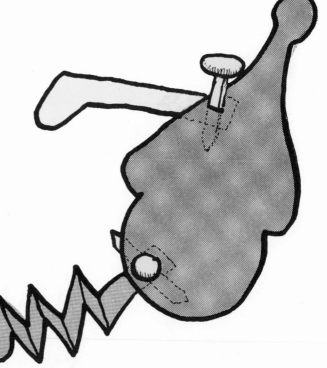

Cut the string into four pieces, each about 2 feet (.6 cm) long.

Punch a hole at the end of each arm and each leg. Tie one end of each piece of string through each hole.

Tape the two sticks together to make an X.

Now tape the end of the leg strings to opposite ends of the X. Use the other ends for the arm strings. Be sure to tape the arm strings a little shorter. Then your puppet will stand up.

Hold the X in the middle. Rock the X back and forth. Your space puppet can walk or dance.

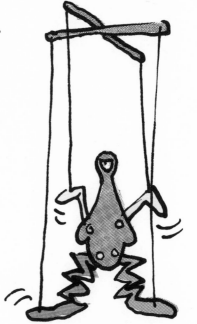

SPACE PUPPET PLAYHOUSE

You can make a space puppet playhouse from any large cardboard box. If you use a very large box, the people who work the puppets can climb inside.

Even a small box will give you a wonderful place to put on puppet shows.

Ask a grown-up to help you cut off the flaps.

Then ask the grown-up to help you cut a large opening in one side.

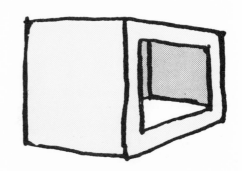

Draw or paint a background scene on the inside of the box. Use foil or cut-out shapes to make the scene more fantastic.

Put the box in between two chairs.

Put a cloth or sheet over the chairs so that no one can see you at work!

Then you are ready to give a show!

GIVING A SPACE PUPPET PLAY

You will need puppets you have made. They will be your cast.

Then you will need a story you and your puppets can act out. This will be your script. You can write the script out, or you can make it up as you go along.

Ask a friend to use a light in your playhouse. Or you can string Christmas tree lights around the outside or inside of your playhouse. These can be your special effects.

Get some whistles, bells, horns, or pieces of wood. You can use these things, alone or together, to make sound effects. They will add to the fun of your play.

Finally, ask some people to watch your play. This will be your audience. You can invite your family and friends to see a

SPECIAL SPACE PUPPET ADVENTURE!